1699

P9-DYJ-743

NORTH HAVEN MEMORIAL LIBRARY
NORTH HAVEN, CT 06473

MAY '07

NORTH HAVEN MEMORIAL LIBRARY
NORTH HAVEN, CT 06473

GOTTA DANCE!

The Rhythms of Jazz and Tap

Jenai Cutcher

rosen
central™

The Rosen Publishing Group, Inc., New York

Special thanks to Maria DiDia

Thanks to Luigi's Jazz Center, New York, NY

Published in 2004 by The Rosen Publishing Group, Inc.
29 East 21st Street, New York, NY 10010

Copyright © 2004 by The Rosen Publishing Group, Inc.

First Edition

All rights reserved. No part of this book may be reproduced in any form
without permission in writing from the publisher, except by a reviewer.

Library of Congress Cataloging-in-Publication Data

Cutcher, Jenai.
　　Gotta dance! : the rhythms of jazz and tap / Jenai Cutcher.
　　p. cm.—(The curtain call library of dance)
　　Summary: Explores the history of jazz and tap dancing, what is involved
　　in becoming a dancer, and what to look for when watching a jazz or tap
　　dancing performance.
　　ISBN 0-8239-4554-5 (lib. bdg.)
　　1. Jazz dance—Juvenile literature. 2. Tap dancing—Juvenile
　　literature. [1. Jazz dance. 2. Tap dancing. 3. Tap dancers. 4.
　　Occupations.] I. Title. II. Series.

GV1784.C88 2004
793.3—dc22

2003011952

Manufactured in the United States of America

CONTENTS

Introduction   4

chapter 1 The Roots of Rhythm   6

chapter 2 A Class of Your Own   14

chapter 3 Staying in Tune With Your Body   22

chapter 4 Watching Jazz and Tap   26

chapter 5 Finding Your Groove   32

Glossary   38

For More Information   40

For Further Reading   42

Bibliography   44

Index   46

INTRODUCTION

Before taking your place behind the curtain, you take a second to make sure the screws on your tap shoes are tight. You are barely able to keep still while the orchestra plays the overture. Onstage, the rest of the cast looks just as anxious and excited as you feel. The first chords to the song "42nd Street" are struck and the curtain rises. As it does, the audience can see each dancer from the knees down. Your feet are drumming out their first time step in your first musical performance. Even before the audience can see the faces of you and your fellow dancers, it is cheering for this grand opening of precise footwork. When the curtain finishes rising, the audience can see

that the excitement has made you just as happy as it has made them.

Whether it's a theatrical tap performance such as this, a rhythm or jazz tap jam, or a jazz number onstage, dancing is a wonderful way to express yourself. It allows your body and mind to work together creatively. Dancing is great exercise and a fun way to make friends.

In this book, we will be taking a closer look at the dazzling world of jazz and tap dance. We're going to learn about getting the most out of dance lessons, taking care of your body, and much more. Our journey through this exciting world begins with the rich history of jazz and tap dance.

● This tap dancer enjoys the spotlight onstage at the Joyce Theater in New York City. The theater is home to a variety of dance performances as well as educational programs.

CHAPTER I

THE ROOTS OF RHYTHM

Jazz and tap dancing are the body "singing." Everything in jazz dancing, from basic steps to advanced choreography, relies on rhythm. Your body makes shapes in order to create a melody of its own. As a tap dancer, your body becomes a percussive instrument, aided by the shoes on your feet and the floor beneath you. You learn how to move your body in different ways in order to produce sound when your shoes hit the floor. This very important relationship between movement and music is the key to learning about tap and jazz dance forms.

Key elements of any type of jazz and tap include syncopation, or the shifting of accents to weak or unexpected beats in the music, individual style, and improvisation. The various styles of jazz dance, including hip-hop, break dancing, and swing dancing, all combine these elements in some way. However, the term jazz dance most directly applies to the theatrical kind of movement seen more on stage, in film, and on television. Tap dancing shares the key elements of jazz dancing. The two main styles of tap dancing are called rhythm or jazz tap and theatrical tap.

Jazz and tap are both American art forms and unique aspects of the nation's culture. Because immigrants from all over the world came to live in America, these dance styles are combinations of many international dance traditions. They both spring most directly from the rich techniques and rhythms of African dance and music. Tap dancing emerged first, jazz dancing came later.

Take It From the Top

In America, traditional dances such as the Irish jig, English clog dancing, and native African dances began to blend together and influence each other as early as the mid-seventeenth century. However, tap dancing as we know it today didn't begin to appear onstage until the minstrel shows of the mid-nineteenth century. These shows grew into what we know as vaudeville. Many of tap dancing's first masters who were rhythm or jazz tap dancers, such as Bill "Bojangles" Robinson, Peg Leg Bates, and Buster Brown, began their careers in vaudeville.

In the end of the nineteenth century and beginning of the twentieth century, tap dancing was greatly influenced by social dances such as the cakewalk and the turkey trot. In the Roaring Twenties, tap

● Legendary tap dancer Buster Brown busts a move during a 1997 performance at Town Hall in New York City.

7

dancing blended with the rhythms of jazz music. This dancing dazzled audiences on Broadway and in Hollywood musicals. Some of the African-American rhythm tap dancers from vaudeville worked in these Hollywood films. However, European-American dancers, such as Fred Astaire, Ann Miller, and the child prodigy Shirley Temple—who blended the footwork of rhythm tap with the upper body style of ballet or ballroom dancing—dominated the silver screen.

Thanks to the work of dancers such as Gregory Hines, Lynn Dally, and Brenda Bufalino, the unique contributions of the great African-American rhythm tap dancers have been rediscovered. The young tap sensation Savion Glover made the funk style of tap dancing, called hittin', popular with dancers who were studying today's tap dancing. Glover traced the African roots of rhythm tap in the Broadway show *Bring in 'Da Noise/Bring in 'Da Funk*. Today, rhythm tap and theatrical tap exist side by side as equally respected styles, coming from the same great roots.

● For over sixty-five years, Fred Astaire dazzled audiences with his graceful dancing. Astaire's name is still one of the most recognizable in the movie business.

Jeni LeGon

One of the first women to make a living as a rhythm tap dancer was Jeni LeGon. In the 1930s, when tap dance acts were popular in the vaudeville circuit shows, most women performed as members of the chorus. This is where LeGon got her start when she was about fifteen years old. It wasn't long before she exchanged the chorus line skirt for a pair of pants and flat shoes. At a time when most of the solo tap dance acts were men, LeGon established herself as a solo tap artist. She performed all the moves the men did, like flips, spins, splits, and toe stands. Jeni LeGon was the first African-American woman to sign a long-term contract with a major Hollywood studio. She was also the only African-American woman to dance with Bill Robinson in film.

● In 1934, Katherine Dunham began one of the most successful dance careers in theater. She went on to leading roles in musicals, operas, and cabarets throughout the world.

All That Jazz

Jazz dancing has a somewhat different history. The African-American anthropologist and dancer Katherine Dunham began choreographing African and Caribbean-based theatrical dances in New York in 1939. Her career spanned many years and included works for Broadway, Hollywood, and the concert stage. In 1940, the Russian-born ballet dancer

George Balanchine choreographed the Broadway show *Cabin in the Sky*, featuring Dunham and her company as dancers. His ballet, *Slaughter on Tenth Avenue*, which was choreographed for the Broadway musical *On Your Toes* in 1936, is thought by some dance historians to be one of the earliest examples of American theatrical jazz dancing.

Fancy Free, a ballet about three sailors on leave in New York City, choreographed by Jerome Robbins in 1944, also combined ballet and jazz dancing. It was the basis for the Broadway musical and film *On the Town*. In 1957, Robbins conceived, directed,

● In the 1930s and early 1940s, George Balanchine choreographed musical comedies on Broadway. His choreography for these shows became famous because of the way he used classical ballet and jazz together.

11

and choreographed *West Side Story* using the dynamic rhythms of jazz dancing to tell the story of a war between two New York City street gangs. Bob Fosse introduced his provocative jazz style to Broadway in the 1954 musical, *The Pajama Game*. *Sweet Charity* (1965), *Chicago* (1975), and *All That Jazz* (1979) all attest to the great popularity of Fosse's slinky, unsentimental style.

● Luigi (front center) teaches his jazz technique to a new generation of jazz dancers.

Jazz dancing, in many forms, dominates the Broadway stage today. Susan Stroman used swing dancing in *Contact*, her award-winning dance-theater show about personal relationships. Twyla Tharp combined ballet, modern and jazz to tell the story of a group of friends torn apart by the Vietnam War in the Broadway musical set to music by Billy Joel, *Movin' Out*.

A Jazz Dance Master

Eugene Louis Fuccuito, known as Luigi, is said to be the first jazz dancer to create a specific technique for teaching theatrical jazz dancing. Shortly after returning from World War II, Luigi was in a car accident in Hollywood that left him so injured that doctors told him he would never walk again. His determination to return to dancing pushed him to create stretches and exercises to get his body back in shape. He was soon teaching his exercises to others. What began as personal physical therapy became the Luigi Jazz Technique.

13

CHAPTER 2
A CLASS OF YOUR OWN

Taking a tap or jazz dance class can be a fun way to learn about dance history, get great exercise and express yourself with your friends. Dance classes might be offered at your school, a community center in your area, or a local dance studio.

Gearing Up

Just as you need certain supplies for school, like paper and pencils, dance class also requires you to come prepared. Part of your preparation means being dressed properly.

The clothes you wear to class should allow you to move easily. Whether you choose shirts, tank tops, leotards, pants, shorts, or tights, it is very important for you to feel comfortable. Your teacher may want you to wear a particular type of clothes to class. This will help him or her see your body and your movements more clearly.

Having the right shoes for class is important too. Be sure to check with your teacher to make sure you get the right style for your class. Tap and jazz shoes come in many different styles, depending on the type of dance you do. Oxfords, sneakers, and pull-on boots are the most common styles of jazz shoes today. Tap shoes can be oxford-style or character-style. The taps—aluminum or metal plates—are attached with screws to the bottom of the shoes at the toes and heels. Some taps can be

● Tap dance footwear comes in a variety of styles. In the lower left corner are tap shoes with taps. In the upper right corner is a jazz boot.

"tuned" by adjusting the screws in the taps. When Savion Glover starred in *The Tap Dance Kid* (1983), he started a trend of adding taps to sneakers.

Being Your Best

The dance studio is your classroom. By being on your best behavior, you can help make it a place where you can learn and have fun at the same time. Respect your teacher and follow his or her directions. If you are dancing or talking while your teacher is instructing the class, you may miss something—so pay attention. Teachers often suggest corrections or helpful tips on how to do certain steps. This is a vital part of the learning process. Even if it is hard at first, taking these corrections and trying to do what is asked will make you a better dancer.

Listening is the key to taking a tap or jazz class. Remember that you are a

Fun Fact

Your dance training can help you do well in school. Numerous studies agree that dancers as a group are more goal-oriented than their non-dancing peers!

dancer *and* a musician. Learning how to make rhythms with your body requires you to listen carefully to the music, your teacher, and yourself. A good student and dancer always has good listening skills.

Tap and Jazz Rhythms

You will learn a lot about music in a tap or jazz class. You will become familiar with concepts like beats, bars, and tempo. You will learn how to count beats in music so you know when to do each step in a sequence. Tap and jazz dance are very closely related to jazz music, so listening to jazz music will greatly inform your dancing. Eventually, you will be able to distinguish different styles of music, such as swing, funk, Latin, hip-hop, and bebop.

Inside or outside of class, the more you listen to the music, the more you will understand it and be able to interpret it through dance.

One tradition of jazz music is call and response. This is very similar to having a conversation with another person. For example, you might say, "Hello," to a friend and ask, "How are you?" Your friend might answer, "Just fine. How are you?" and you would answer back. The same type of exchange can happen as a danced conversation with your whole body in jazz class, or just your feet in tap class.

Many tap and jazz teachers use a similar format to communicate new rhythms to their students. Just as you learn how to speak a phrase in a foreign language by listening to it and repeating it several times, you can learn new steps and rhythms by echoing what your teacher does.

Tap and Jazz Lingo

Class is also the place to learn the names of common steps and how to do them correctly. Each style of dance has a specific vocabulary. Jazz dance shares many terms with ballet, like pas de bourrée (boo-**ray**) and battement (bat-**mont**), but you will also learn about isolations, hitch kicks, and pivot turns. These movements are learned and practiced as part of exercises. Basic tap steps include steps, brushes, and scuffs. They can be combined in different ways to make more complex movements, like shuffles, flaps, and pull backs. These steps and others like them are the building blocks that dancers use to form an entire phrase or sequence of movements and sounds.

That's the Way It Goes

No matter what the style, a jazz or tap dance class usually follows a certain progression, from warm-up to technique exercises to learning a combination. This progression helps to prevent injuries and trains your mind and body to work together. For example, your jazz class may start with knee bends called pliés (plee-**ayz**), or movements of certain parts of your body like your hips or ribs called isolations. These movements can be followed by other repetitive actions to warm up all the muscles in your body. These warm-up exercises, which are usually performed in one place, prepare your body for the turns, leaps, and movements at faster tempos that travel across the floor.

The last portion of class is often reserved for learning a routine, or a long combination choreographed by your teacher. It is your opportunity to put together everything

● These jazz dancers are doing a combination in class. Practicing routines such as this is a great way to learn your teacher's technique.

you've been practicing in class. The routine is set to a certain piece of music and involves the whole class dancing together. Many dance schools end the year with a recital, a performance that allows you to dance your routine on a stage. It's your chance to show your family and friends in the audience what you have been learning.

Sometimes tap or jazz classes include time to improvise. Improvisation is dancing in the moment—you are making up what you're doing as you go along. Like choreography, improvisation or simply, "improv" is a chance to use what you know and put steps together in a different way. Unlike choreography, it is not planned out ahead of time. Improvisation is a skill. Improvement comes from practicing in the same way you practice a new step. The more you do it, the easier it will become. Improvising is a chance to express your own individual style and a fun way to learn more about your classmates.

● Improvisation is a fun way to use the new steps you have learned to create a dance of your own.

Talk the Talk

The language of jazz and tap dance is filled with many fascinating terms. Here's a brief list of some of them:

battement - literally translated from French, it means beat, but in jazz class, it usually means a big brush or kick of the leg

brush - swinging the leg so that the ball of the foot hits the floor

flap - a brush forward followed immediately with a shift of weight to the ball of the same foot

hitch kick - flicking one leg while the other one passes, shooting into the air

pas de bourrée - simple connecting steps used to link other steps in combination

pivot turn - a step in one direction, followed quickly by a twist of the whole body usually 180°, to a new direction

pull back - series of weight shifts to make one jump beginning with a brush back with the right foot, then the left followed with a landing onto the right foot, then the left

scuff - swinging the leg so that the heel hits the floor

shuffle - a brush forward followed immediately with a brush back

CHAPTER 3
STAYING IN TUNE WITH YOUR BODY

Listening to your body is very important. To do your best in dance class or rehearsals, you must always take care of your body. This means maintaining a healthy diet and getting plenty of sleep. Being physically active takes a lot of strength and energy. Giving your body the nutrients and sleep it needs will keep you from getting tired. Many injuries happen when a dancer feels too tired or weak. Being good to your body can have many positive effects, long into the future.

What Your Body Needs

Dancers are like athletes and an athlete's body needs the right fuel to keep it going.

Make sure that your body gets what it needs by eating healthy foods. Fruits and vegetables, fish, meats, nuts, whole grains, and dairy or soy products will provide you with the right mix of protein, carbohydrates, and other nutrients you need.

Every body is different and needs different things, so a diet that works for you may not be what's best for your classmate. In fact, it is quite normal for your own health needs to change as your body develops. What works for you now might not always work.

It's a good idea to discuss health choices with your doctor, teachers, and parents.

Proper hygiene is essential for any serious student. It is always important to keep yourself and your clothes neat

● Fruit has both vitamins and nutrients that are good for your body. The natural sugars of fruit are a great source of energy.

and clean. As your body changes you may also need to use deodorant. This is especially true for hard workouts that can make you sweat.

Times of rapid growth and change also mean that things you do in dance class may begin to feel different. This may sometimes feel strange or confusing, but try to "go with the flow." These changes are all very natural and are exciting aspects of your development as a dancer and a person.

Working Your Body

In order to keep your muscles conditioned and limber, stretching regularly is a good idea. If you do this on your own, try listening to different kinds of music every time you stretch, so you are working out in two ways at once.

Yoga is a series of exercises that help develop control of the body and mind. Practicing yoga is another way to stretch and tone your muscles. Yoga is great for your circulatory, respiratory, and digestive systems, as well as a good tool to help you relax.

It's in the Bag!

Here are a few important items you may want to have in your dance bag:
shoes
bottle of water
snack (such as a piece of fruit or granola bar)
socks
tights
towel
Band-Aids
screwdriver (for your tap screws)
hair supplies
deodorant

24

Taking a ballet class can also be useful, especially if you are a jazz dancer. Lots of jazz moves are similar to, or based

● Many of the more dramatic jazz moves use the balance and flexibility that ballet dancing helps to build.

on, ballet steps. Ballet can improve your turn-out, flexibility, and balance.

Even though you have conditioned, stretched, and warmed up, it is still possible for you to have an accident. If you do injure yourself, remember this is the most important time to be in tune

with what your body needs. If you're hurting, don't push it. See your doctor if you think an injury might be serious. If you follow the advice of your

teacher, doctor, and parents you will soon be dancing again. In the meantime, you can learn a lot from watching class. You can even use your mind to help train your body, by imagining yourself doing the new moves you observe. If you really see yourself doing each move in rhythm, in your imagination, you will be surprised by how much your body will remember when you are healthy enough to begin dancing again!

25

CHAPTER 4
WATCHING JAZZ AND TAP

Seeing others dance will inspire you and influence your own style. Watching professionals with expert technique and impressive creativity can show you what is possible with continued hard work.

Dance on Television

Turn on your television and you're likely to see tap and jazz dance in some form. Whether it's a bunch of people swing dancing in the latest spring colors or tap legend Gregory Hines showing us how easy it is to make home movies on a computer, TV commercials often use jazz or tap dance themes.

Television stations with arts programming often broadcast shows that are specifically about dance. Documentaries

Fun Fact

The Show Must Go On . . . and On. Some of the longest-running musicals on Broadway were filled with tap and jazz dance performances. They are:

A Chorus Line - June 25, 1975 to April 28, 1990; 6,137 shows

Cats - October 7, 1982 to September 10, 2000; 7,485 shows

about dance history, certain dance styles, or famous dancers and choreographers can expose you to new ideas and information. Live performances by dance companies are sometimes broadcast on television, too.

● Maurice Hines (left) taps with his brother Gregory in the Broadway musical *Sophisticated Ladies*.

Many jazz and hip-hop moves appear in music videos. Sometimes the singers perform these moves themselves, but professional dancers are often hired to compliment the songs with movement. Instructional videos, made by master teachers and professionals like Bob Rizzo and Cathy Roe, are readily available. Watching these videos and trying to do what they teach is a good chance to check out the other jazz or tap styles.

Dance in the Movies

Movies offer jazz and tap dance in many forms. Many movie musicals such as *Flying Down to Rio* and *Orchestra Wives* are famous for their dance scenes. In the title number from the Hollywood musical *Singin' in the Rain*, dancer and choreographer Gene Kelly mixed the sounds of rain splashing with the rhythmic patterns of his tap dancing to create one of the best-loved dance sequences of all time. Many Broadway musicals that feature jazz or tap dancing have also been turned into movies. These include *West Side Story*, *Cabaret*, and *The Wiz*. You can pick up these movies at a video rental store.

Sometimes the primary subject of a movie is dance and all the main characters are dancers. *Fame* is a movie about students at a performing arts high school. You can see the dancers in their classes, performing, and just hanging out and dancing in the streets. Gregory Hines is the star of the movie *Tap*, appearing with many of rhythm tap's original masters. In the famous challenge scene, Hines jams with the great hoofers Harold Nicholas, Bunny Briggs, Sandman Sims, Steve Condos, Sammy Davis, Jr., and Jimmy Slyde.

Live Dance

Nothing captures the pulsing energy of dance like a live performance. Opportunities to see dance probably exist

● George Chakiris leads dancers down a New York City street in a scene from *West Side Story*.

● This production of *Tap Dogs* brought down the house at Sadlers Wells Theatre in London, England.

right in your area, especially if you live in or near a big city. Community theater companies sometimes perform musicals that include tap or jazz dance. Many colleges and universities have dance departments that produce concerts throughout the school year. Some major cities have tap or jazz dance companies in residence or special dance events, like Tap City, in New York.

Dance Companies and Events

There are many famous dance companies and events in the United States. Here are a few of the best known:

Buraczeski's Jazzdance - Minneapolis/St. Paul, Minnesota
Hubbard Street Dance - Chicago, Illinois
Jazz Tap Ensemble - Los Angeles, California
Manhattan Tap - New York, New York
Portsmouth Percussive Dance - Portsmouth, New Hampshire

The **Jazz Dance World Congress** is an annual five-day event celebrating jazz dance. It is sponsored by the Gus Giordano Dance Company and School. The event gathers dancers, teachers, and performers from across the United States and from as many as thirty-five foreign countries. At the event, these jazz dance enthusiasts take classes from world-class master teachers, see performances by internationally known dance companies, witness the judging of new jazz dance choreography, and discuss any topic of interest to jazz dancers.

CHAPTER 5
FINDING YOUR GROOVE

You can decide how seriously you wish to take your dancing, and continue to train accordingly. There are as many options open to you as you can imagine. Be sure that you are doing what's right for you.

Taking It to the Next Level

Your parents and dance instructors can help you with making choices. When it comes to planning your future, your parents can offer their guidance and support. Asking your dance teacher for advice can provide great benefits. He or she can evaluate your skills and technique level, offer suggestions for improvement, and help you set goals for your develop-ment. Dance teachers are also helpful with providing resources for you, such as summer workshops, college, and audition information.

Seeking out performance opportunities is one way to gain experience as a dancer. Whether it's dancing in your studio's year-end recital or participating in your school's shows, performing is an experience the classroom can't provide. Being in cos-tume and onstage sharing your dancing with an audi-ence is an exciting way to challenge yourself and grow as a dancer. Being in a show lets you see what happens behind the scenes, too. It takes many people doing many jobs to put a show together.

● Dance teachers work hard to help you in the classroom. They can also be a great guide for finding you dance opportunities outside the studio.

Different Beats

There are many ways to participate in the world of jazz and tap without dancing. A performance needs costumes, music, lights, sound, publicity, and many other things that are often handled by dancers who have talent in these areas. You can apply other talents or develop other interests while contributing to dance performances as part of the creative team behind the scenes.

Creating dances is another aspect of study that you can consider as you progress as a dancer. If you like making up your own moves, try choreographing a dance for yourself or some friends. Many of the names mentioned in this book and several other famous jazz and tap dancers have also worked as choreographers and directors.

Opportunities to be involved in dance are increasing all the time. Have you ever considered writing about the dance performances you see? You could share

● Whether it's a retro-1950s hoop skirt or an elegant tuxedo, costumes add to the drama of a dance performance.

● Choreographing a dance for yourself allows you to add a new level of expression to your dancing.

your opinions as a dance writer or critic. If you enjoy communicating what you know to others, perhaps teaching dance is right for you. With changes in technology, dance on film is becoming more popular.

National Tap Dance Day

The birthday of Bill "Bojangles" Robinson, May 25th, was officially declared National Tap Dance Day in 1989. In honor of this day, dozens of special events and celebrations of dance are held throughout the United States.

Directing or editing these projects could be fun, too.

The possibilities in jazz and tap are endless, but it is important to remember that dancing, when taken seriously, becomes a large part of your lifestyle. It requires a lot of hard work and dedication, even when you're not in class. Most importantly, you must love to do it—that's when you can really groove.

● Bill "Bojangles" Robinson started his career as a boy dancing for pennies in the street. He went on to star in vaudeville and onstage. He also appeared in fourteen movies.

GLOSSARY

bars (**barz**) The measures or groups of beats in a piece of music.

beat (**beet**) The regular rhythm of music or movement.

choreography (kor-ee-**og**-ruh-fee) The art of creating and arranging dance movements.

flexibility (**flek**-suh-buhl-ete) The degree to which you can stretch your muscles.

improvisation (im-prov-uh-**zay**-shuhn) Making up material on the spot.

isolations (**eye**-suh-late-shuhnz) Moving a single body part by itself.

minstrel (**min**-struhl) A variety show of blackface performers.

percussive (pur-**kuhs**-iv) Musically hitting one thing against another.

recital (ri-**sye**-tuhl) A performance by a solo or group of performing artists such as dancers or musicians.

syncopation (**sink**-oh-pay-shuhn) Accenting weak or unexpected beats.

technique (tek-**neek**) A method or way of doing something that requires skill.

tempo (**tem**-poh) The speed or timing of a piece of music or dance.

turn-out (**turn-out**) The degree of outward rotation of your legs in your hip sockets.

vaudeville (**vaw**-de-vil) A stage show with various acts of song, dance, and comedy.

FOR MORE INFORMATION

Organizations

American Tap Dance Foundation
33 Little West 12th Street
Suite #105B
New York, NY 10014
(646) 638-4518
Web site: http://www.tapdancing.org

American Institute of Vernacular Jazz Dance
34 West 129th Street
Suite 5A
New York, NY 10027
(212) 353-7265
Web site: http://www.aivjd.org

Web Sites

Due to the changing nature of Internet links, the Rosen Publishing Group, Inc., has developed an online list of Web sites related to the subject of this book. This site is updated regularly. Please use this link to access the list:

http://www.rosenlinks.com/ccld/jazztap/

FOR FURTHER READING

Books

Feldman, Anita. *Inside Tap: Technique and Improvisation for Today's Tap Dancer*. Hightstown, NJ: Princeton Book Company, 1996.

Frank, Rusty E. *Tap: The Greatest Tap Dance Stars and Their Stories 1900-1955*. New York: Da Capo Press, 1995.

Giordano, Gus. *Jazz Dance Class: Beginning Thru Advanced*. Hightstown, NJ: Princeton Book Company, 1992.

Gottfried, Martin. *All His Jazz: The Life and Death of Bob Fosse*. New York: Da Capo Press, 1998.

Gray, Acia. *The Souls of Your Feet: A Tap Dance Guidebook for Rhythm Explorence*: Austin, TX: Grand Weaver's Publishing, 1998.

Johnson, Anne E. *Jazz Tap: From African Drums to American Feet*. New York: Rosen Publishing Group, 1999.

Magazines and Publications

Curtain Call Dance Club Revue
P.O. Box 709
York, PA 17405-0709
Web site: http://www.cckids.com

Dance
333 7th Avenue, 11th floor
New York, NY 10001
(212) 979-4803
Web site: http://www.dancemagazine.com

Dancer
2829 Bird Avenue, Suite 5 PMB 231
Miami, FL 33133
(305) 460-3225
Web site: http://www.danceronline.com

Dance Spirit
Lifestyle Ventures, LLC.
250 West 57th Street, Suite 420
New York, NY 10107
(212) 265-8890
Web site: http://www.dancespirit.com

BIBLIOGRAPHY

Frank, Rusty E. *Tap: The Greatest Tap Dance Stars and Their Stories 1900-1955*. New York: Da Capo Press, 1995.

Knowles, Mark. *Tap Roots: The Early History of Tap Dancing*. Jefferson, NC: McFarland and Company Incorporated Publishers, 2002.

Luigi, Lorraine Person Kriegel, and Francis James Roach. *Luigi's Jazz Warm Up: An Introduction to Jazz Style and Technique*. Hightstown, NJ: Princeton Book Company, 1997.

Stearns, Marshall and Jean. *Jazz Dance: The Story of American Vernacular Dance*. New York: Da Capo Press, 1994.

INDEX

A

Astaire, Fred, 8

B

Balanchine, George, 11
bars, 17
Bates, Peg Leg, 7
battement, 18, 21
beat, 6, 17, 34
Brown, Buster, 7
Bufalino, Brenda, 8

C

call and response, 17
choreography, 6, 20
circulatory, 24

D

Dally, Lynn, 8
Dunham, Katherine, 10, 11

F

flexibility, 25
Fosse, Bob, 11, 12
Fuccuito, Eugene Louis, 12, 13

G

Glover, Savion, 8, 16

H

Hines, Gregory, 8, 26, 28
hygiene, 23

I

improvisation, 6, 20
isolations, 18

K

Kelly, Gene, 28

L

LeGon, Jeni, 9

M

Miller, Ann, 8
minstrel, 7

N

Nicholas, Harold, 28

O
orchestra, 4, 28

P
pas de bourrée, 18
percussive, 6
performance, 4–5, 20, 26, 28, 32, 34
pliés, 18
provocative, 12

R
recital, 20, 32
rehearsal, 22
respiratory, 24
rhythm, 4, 6–8, 28
Robbins, Jerome, 11–12
Robinson, Bill "Bojangles", 7, 9, 36

S
Stroman, Susan, 13
syncopation, 6

T
technique, 7, 18, 26, 32
Temple, Shirley, 8
tempo, 17, 19
Tharp, Twyla, 13
turn-out, 25

V
vaudeville, 7–9, 36

Y
yoga, 24

About the Author

Originally from Ohio, Jenai Cutcher is a tap dancer, choreographer, teacher, and writer based in New York City.

Photo Credits: Cover © Everett Collection; pp. 1, 9, 13, 15, 21, 24, 25, 31, 34, 35, 36 © Simone Associates, Lebanon, PA; pp. 5, 7 © Julie Lemberger/Corbis; pp. 8, 10, 11, 27, 29, 37 © Bettmann/Corbis; pp. 12, 16, 19 courtesy Luigi's Jazz Center/photographer: Milton Oleaga; p. 20 © Zigy Kaluzny/Getty Images; pp. 22–23 © Comstock; p. 30 © Robbie Jack/Corbis; p. 33 courtesy of Susan Epstein

Editor: Kevin Somers **Book Design:** Christopher Logan and Erica Clendening

Developmental Editors: Nancy Allison, CMA, RME, and Susan Epstein

j792.78   Cutcher, Jenai
Cutcher
           Gotta Dance!

**NORTH HAVEN
MEMORIAL LIBRARY**
NORTH HAVEN, CT 06473